Feed
the Baby

Jessica Egbert

Photo credit: bigstockphoto.com
Cover design by: Alaka Oladimeji

ISBN: 0-578-43882-8
ISBN-13: 978-0-578-43882-5

Published by Obstruction Press

DEDICATION

Thank you to my son, who inspired this book with his curious questions about his new sister. To all the mamas and daddies out there- you are doing a great job raising your child. Just remember, there is more than one way to do things.

What do baby animals eat?

Mammals are a type of animal that drink milk from their mothers.

A calf drinks mama's milk.

A puppy drinks mama's milk.

A fawn drinks mama's milk.

A baby drinks mama's milk.

Mammals nurse their young for different lengths of time, between 3 days and 8 years.

The little ones begin eating other types of food as they grow older, like meat or vegetables.

How do baby animals eat?

Mammals have special organs called breasts and nipples. Mothers produce milk inside of their breasts.

Milk flows out of the nipple to feed the baby. Boys do have nipples, but not the kind for feeding babies.

Breasts and nipples have lots of names.
Animal nipples are often called teats.

Breasts are sometimes called boobs or boobies.

Babies drink milk from a bottle.

Formula can be used in a bottle.

Mama's milk can be used in a bottle.

No matter how a baby eats, the most important thing is that the baby is fed!

Fun Facts

Mammals get their name from the Latin word for breast, "mamma."

Male and female mammals have mammary glands, but they grow differently in females and produce milk in mothers.

A platypus mother does not have nipples. The babies drink milk that drips out of glands (similar to how we sweat).

Male mice and horses do not have teats.

Hooded seal pups drink their mother's milk for only 3-5 days, while orangutans can nurse for 8 or 9 years!

Most formula contains cow's milk.

The first infant formulas were sold starting in the 1860s.

Made in the USA
San Bernardino, CA
14 January 2019